The Rose Island Lighthouse Series

THE ISLAND ADVENTURES OF PAUL STEDMAN

Lynne Heinzmann
Robin Roraback
Michaela Fournier
Marilyn Harris

Norwalk, Connecticut

Copyright © 2021 by Lynne Heinzmann

All rights reserved. No part of the book may be reproduced in any form or by any electronic or mechanical means, including information storage and retrieval systems, without written permission from the publisher, except by a reviewer who may quote passages for review.

Library of Congress Cataloguing-in-Publication Data available

Paperback - 978-1-949116-47-2

First Edition

TABLE OF CONTENTS

Introduction	4	*Coffee Trading*	38
Paul Arrives at the Lighthouse	6	Newport Naval Torpedo Station	42
Jesse Orton	10	*A Strange Visitor*	44
The Island Ladies	12	Fall River Line	48
The Great Depression	18	*Poems with Gramp*	50
The Rusty Stove	20	Entertainment in the 1930s	54
Life in the 1930s	24	*Fireworks with Mamma and Pappa*	56
Keeping the Light Burning	26	Rose Island Lighthouse & Fort Hamilton Trust	60
Fresnel Lens	30	The Book Team	61
A Foggy Night	32	Picture Credits	62
Fog Signals	36		

INTRODUCTION

In 1870, just after the Civil War, a lighthouse was completed on Rose Island, an 18-acre isle of marsh grass in Narragansett Bay, half-way between Jamestown and Newport, Rhode Island. The wood-framed building guided boats through the bay and warned them of the rocky shoals north of Newport Harbor. The lighthouse's 8-sided tower housed a Fresnel lens that shot a beam of light 48 feet above the 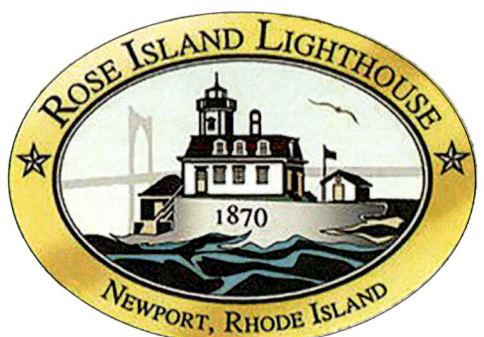 water. The Coast Guard took over the operation of the Rose Island Lighthouse in 1939 and ran it until 1971 when the light was decommissioned, deemed unnecessary because of the completion of the nearby Newport Bridge. The property was eventually turned over to the General Services Administration who offered it at no cost to the City of Newport in 1984. In 1985, the lighthouse was adopted by the Rose Island Lighthouse Foundation who oversaw its revitalization, and made it into the wonderful living museum it is today.

A few years ago, the Lighthouse Foundation—now called the Rose Island Lighthouse and Fort Hamilton Trust—was looking for a way to increase public awareness of Rose Island, furnish factual information to students going there on field trips, and provide a keepsake for visitors to purchase at the island's giftshop. The group commissioned a series of books, each covering a different era of the building's storied history. In 2019, Woodhall Press published the first book of the series, The Curious Childhood of Wanton Chase, which discussed the history of the lighthouse around 1915, just before World War I. The book you now hold in your hands is the second volume of the series and covers the history of the lighthouse in the 1930s, during the Great Depression before World War II.

As a boy, Paul Stedman lived with his grandfather, Jesse Orton, the keeper at the Rose Island Lighthouse, and with Charlie Eldridge, the assistant keeper. Paul stayed there full-time in the early 1930s when he was six and seven years old and then visited the island nearly every summer for the rest of his childhood. Later in life, he recorded his memories of his adventures on the island. The story chapters in this book are based upon these recollections. The alternating history chapters contain information and period photographs to further explain the stories and reveal more about life there in the 1930s. We hope you enjoy reading this book about Paul and learning more about the Rose Island Lighthouse.

Paul Stedman and Jesse Orton, 1933

Rose Island Lighthouse, 1934

PAUL ARRIVES AT THE LIGHTHOUSE

Even though Paul was only five years old, when he was called into the lighthouse's kitchen that sunny day in May 1931, he could tell that something big was about to happen. His mamma, pappa, grandpa, and the assistant lighthouse keeper, Charlie, were all sitting in the yellow chairs, crowded around the kitchen table, with very serious looks on their faces. For a moment, Paul wondered if he'd done something bad—really bad—that had made all of these grown-ups mad at him, but then his mamma smiled and reached out her arms. "Please come over here, Paul," she said. He climbed into her lap and snuggled against her soft white dress that smelled like the ocean. "Grandpa Orton has something he'd like to talk to you about," she said. "I want you to listen to him very carefully."

Paul turned to face his grandpa, who was seated closest to the window, the bright sunlight glinting off the gold buttons of his blue keeper's uniform. Paul liked Gramp very much. He was always kind and friendly and spent time playing games and going for walks along the beach with Paul every time the boy and his family took the train up from New York City to visit.

"Well, Paul," Gramp said, "as you know, your Grandma Orton passed away a few months ago."

Paul nodded solemnly. He missed Gram's soft hands, smiling face, gentle laugh, and the lemon cookies that she had baked and stored in one of the lighthouse kitchen's drawers. When they'd arrived for their visit this time, Paul had opened that drawer to find only a few stale crumbs in the corners.

Gramp said, "With her gone, it's just Charlie and me here at the lighthouse, two old bachelors." He patted the assistant keeper on the shoulder of his uniform, which had far fewer gold buttons that Gramp's did. "We were wondering if you might like to come and stay with us for a while."

Paul frowned with confusion. "Stay with you, sir?"

His grandpa nodded. "You'd live out here on the island year-round, to help us run the lighthouse, cook, clean, and do all the other things we need to do to keep this place shipshape."

Paul's eyes opened wide. "You mean I wouldn't have to go to school?"

Gramp chuckled—a warm, rumbly sound. "I'm afraid you'd still have to go to school. It'd be a different one, though, the school in Newport. You could ride over there every morning on the boat that picks up the Marines from their nighttime guard duty shift and then Charlie could fetch you in the lighthouse's launch after school to bring you back here to the island."

"I'd get to take a boat to school and back every day?" Paul asked. "That would be fun!"

"And it'll be nice to have another young man around," Charlie joked. To Paul, Charlie looked older than Paul's pappa and just a little younger than Gramp. "And besides," the assistant keeper added, "I could certainly use some help lugging those big, heavy kerosene buckets up to the tower and down to the foghorn room."

"Aw hush, Charlie. You're going to scare the boy," Gramp said with a smile. "Paul, there'd be a lot of fun things to do,

like polish the lantern, milk the cow, and play with the other children who live here on the island. You already know Georgie and Freddie, Sargent Miller's kids." Paul had been playing with the Marine's boys earlier that morning.

Gramp nodded toward Paul's parents. "Of course, you wouldn't see much of your mamma or pappa. But don't forget you'd be helping them out, too, by letting the United States Government pay to feed you during this Depression." He chuckled again. "I've seen the way you eat. If you lived here, you'd save your folks a fortune in groceries."

Paul swiveled to look at his parents.

His pappa tousled Paul's short brown hair. "We'd come up to see you whenever we could, sport—holidays and long weekends—whenever I have some time off work." Francis Stedman was an important man selling suits to businessmen in New York City.

"And I'd visit even more often than that," his mamma said. "Aunt Ruth and I could take the train up together once a month or so." She gave him a little hug. "But you'd be having such a good time here with Gramp and Charlie, you probably wouldn't even miss us."

Paul chewed on his lower lip and considered his options. "How long would this be for?"

Gramp said, "How about a year? That way you'll see the island in summer, fall, winter, and spring, and will get a true picture of what it's like being here."

Paul felt everyone in the kitchen staring at him, even Buddy, Gramp's German Shepherd, who was resting in his usual spot under the table. Paul looked from face to face to face and then nodded. "Yes, I'll do it," he said.

His mamma hugged him again, looking a little sad. "That's my big boy. I'm very proud of you and I know you'll be a great help to Gramp and Charlie."

Gramp extended a hand. "Welcome aboard, Paul."

Paul placed his tiny pink hand in his grandpa's big square one and wondered what the next year was going to be like for him, living here at the Rose Island Lighthouse.

JESSE ORTON

Paul's grandfather, Jesse Orton, lived a full and interesting life. He married three times, had two daughters, and worked a variety of jobs: textile worker, military band member, volunteer fireman, machinist, and finally lighthouse keeper. Shortly before he retired from the United States Lighthouse Service in 1936, he wrote this brief memoir of his life:

Lighthouse Keeper Orton, 1916

I was born in the year 1866, in the town of Shrewsbury, Shropshire, England, near the River Severn… But in 1882, my parents came to the United States and with eight children settled in Providence, R. I., and there is where my life really began.

In April 1888, in the Supreme Court at Providence, I was made a citizen of the United States, and in 1892, I enlisted for three years in the Rhode Island Militia. I was also a member of the First Light Infantry… For a few years, I played with the Parks Continental Band in Providence… [One time we] went with a Grand Army Post from Providence to Norwich, Conn., where I got to shake hands with Rutherford B. Hayes, the nineteenth President of the United States.

I was married [to Martha Oates] in 1893, and we went to live in the town of Johnston. [We had two daughters, Alice in 1895 and Ruth in 1901. Martha died shortly after Ruth was born. A few years later, I married Elizabeth Tunnicliffe and she raised the girls as if they were her own.] I worked for some years in the mills, then I worked at Gorham Silver Works, also at Brown and Sharp Mfg. Co.

In 1911, I entered the U.S. Lighthouse Service. My first appointment was [as Assistant Keeper] of Penfield Reef Lighthouse near Bridgeport, Conn. And my recollection of that winter was dreary and drab as the weeks passed slowly by. The following month of May I went to Fire Island Lighthouse and remained through the Summer months. My next place was Shinnecock Lighthouse on Long Island, named after a tribe of Indians who lived in those parts of Long Island. In 1916, I was appointed keeper of the Lighthouse at Crown Point, New York, on the shore of Lake Champlain.

In 1921, I came to Rose Island in Newport Harbor, Rhode Island. In this harbor, the U.S. Navy makes an annual visit in the Summer. It is also the scene of many international boat races and the annual gathering-place for many yacht clubs. [Sadly, my wife died at Rose Island in 1931. A few months later, my grandson, Paul, came to live with me and Charlie Eldridge, my assistant keeper, to help us with some of our minor chores.]

In 1936, I expect to be relieved of all active duty and spend my declining days in retirement. For many years I have kept the light that guides the ships that pass in the night, and as I venture into the great unknown, I wonder will the Lighthouse shine on me?

And so, the Keeper 'tends the light in yonder far off tower,
And guides the mariner on his way to the haven of his heart's desire.

Jesse Orton

After his retirement in 1936, Jesse moved to Florida and married Elizabeth H. Page, his third wife. They lived in Clearwater until he died in 1957.

On Rose Island with Alice, Ruth, their husbands, and baby Paul, 1927

THE ISLAND LADIES

On the first Saturday in June, Paul and his Grandpa Orton stood on the Rose Island pier and waved goodbye as the lighthouse launch pulled away. Paul's mamma and pappa had accompanied him to the island to drop him off for his year-long stay with Gramp, and now Charlie was returning Paul's parents to Newport to catch their train back to New York. Standing on the gently rocking platform, watching the launch get smaller and smaller in the distance, Paul got a squishy feeling in his stomach as he realized he wouldn't be seeing Mamma and Pappa for a very long time—at least a month.

Gramp patted Paul's shoulder and smiled. "My boy, I don't believe you've met the Island Ladies yet."

Paul frowned. "I know Mrs. Miller and Mrs. Roberts, who live over there." He pointed to the two wooden officers' houses near the big, brick TNT Building. During his visit last month, Paul had played with their children. "They're nice ladies."

"Yes, they are," Gramp said, "but, I'm not talking about them. I'm talking about a group of other ladies. Come with me. I'll introduce you."

Paul trotted to keep up with his grandpa as they crossed the grass field behind the lighthouse. When they approached a newly-painted white shed with green trim and shiny glass windows, Paul heard clucking noises that sounded like… "Chickens?" he guessed. They rounded the corner of the shed and were greeted by a dozen white hens, strutting around inside a fenced-in enclosure.

"Paul," Gramp said, "I'd like you to meet the Island Ladies." He waved toward the chickens. "Ladies, I'd like you to meet my grandson, Paul."

"But, when…how…?"

Gramp smiled. "A few weeks ago, Charlie and I hammered together this chicken coop using some scrap lumber and three old windows we found in the lighthouse's basement. And then last weekend, Charlie's cousin, Harry, a farmer from Exeter, was kind enough to give us these hens. They're pretty young but a few of them are already laying. All week, we've been having fresh eggs for breakfast… quite a treat."

"You keep your own chickens so you can have eggs?" Paul was astonished. "At

home, we buy all our eggs from the corner market. But Mamma said the Depression has made eggs too expensive—25 cents for a dozen—so we don't get them anymore."

Gramp nodded. "That's why Charlie and I built this coop." He nodded toward an adjacent fenced-in area where a black-and-white cow contentedly munched on some grass. "And you've met Bessie, of course." They walked over and scratched the cow's bristly forehead. "Did I ever tell you the story about Bessie's trip out to Rose Island?"

Paul shook his head.

"Well, a couple of years ago, I did some work for a farmer in Middletown, fixed up a hole in his boat for him. As payment, he gave me Bessie, but I had to figure a way to get her out here to the island. You see, the lighthouse launch is too small to carry a cow. Fortunately, Captain John from the Jamestown Ferry agreed to bring Bessie to the island for me, but when the time came, it was low tide, so he wasn't able to get very close to shore. John pulled in as near as he could and gently lowered Bessie into the water. Then he and the passengers on the ferry whistled and banged on the side of the boat while Charlie and I called from the beach, encouraging her to swim ashore. By the time she joined us on the beach, she was tuckered out and just lay there for an entire day and night. But the next day she hopped up, strolled up to this field here, and started munching away on the grass as if nothing had happened."

"I know how to milk Bessie," Paul announced. "Gram showed me last summer."

"That's wonderful, my boy. Why don't we make that one of your chores? From now on, you'll be the official Rose Island cow-milker, making sure we have fresh milk every day, an important part of our diet here on the island."

Paul smiled proudly.

Gramp pointed toward a third fenced-in area on the other side of the field, where plants grew in neat rows. "And you know about our vegetable garden there: corn, beans, squash, cucumbers, tomatoes, onions, and potatoes. I think you helped Grandma Orton with the planting when you were here last spring."

Paul was quiet, thinking about Gram, as they walked back to the chicken enclosure. Looking at the hens, he asked, "What are their names?"

"Don't have any yet," Gramp said. "You can give them names if you'd like."

Paul studied the chickens for a few moments and then pointed at one. "That one has a big, red crown on her head, so we can call her Queenie. And this one has four black dots on her back, so we'll call her Spot." He bent over the wire fence and plucked an egg from another clump of grass, holding it up for Gramp's inspection.

Gramp chuckled. "I can see you are going to be a big help to Charlie and me: the Three Bachelors of Rose Island Lighthouse."

Paul smiled. "And for my first job, I am going to name all of the chickens."

Gramp patted Paul's head. "Good idea."

THE GREAT DEPRESSION

At the time Paul lived with his grandfather at the Rose Island Lighthouse, the entire world was in the midst of the Great Depression, the worst economic slump in modern history. It began after the United States' stock market crashed in the fall of 1929 and continued in some countries until the late 1930s. Throughout the world, port cities were affected because of the drastic decline in world trade, and industrial cities were decimated due to the decreased global demand for manufactured goods like steel and automobiles. Emergent nations suffered because of the decreased demand for farming, forestry, fishing, and mining products, while more-developed countries faced severe hardships due to the lack of markets for their refined goods and technologies. Germany, still reeling from the after-effects of World War I, was among the worst-hit nations. During the Great Depression, its citizens suffered widespread unemployment and starvation that ultimately led to the fall of the Weimar Republic, the rise of Adolf Hitler's Nazi Party, and the onset of World War II.

In the United States following the stock market crash of 1929, almost half of the nation's banks collapsed. With their investments and savings gone, consumers spent their money only on necessities. In a chain reaction, many companies failed, which threw 25% of Americans out of work and caused them to lose their homes and possessions. A multi-year drought aggravated by poor environmental practices in a region from southeast Colorado to Texas created the Dust Bowl, which further intensified the nation's economic devastation and food shortages, as thousands of farmers and migrant workers fled that barren area.

President Herbert Hoover badly underestimated the seriousness of the Great Depression and assured everyone that the country's economy would rebound within two months of the stock market crash. When it became obvious that Hoover was wrong and was doing little to resolve the worsening crisis, the American people voted him out of office, electing Franklin Roosevelt by a landslide in the 1932 presidential race. Roosevelt immediately declared a four-day bank holiday and oversaw the implementation of the Emergency Banking Relief Act that stabilized the banking system. Then, he quickly introduced his New Deal, a system of programs and initiatives that eventually allowed the country to recover from the Great Depression.

In Rhode Island, textile mills had been experiencing a steady economic decline for over a decade and the Great Depression only added to the problem. By late 1932, the number of mill workers in the state was 33% of what it had been during the peak employment period just a few decades earlier. As in the rest of the country, other Rhode Island industrial sectors, trades, retailers, and even white-collar jobs were also hit hard. Projects funded by the Work Progress Administration (WPA), one of Roosevelt's New Deal programs, employed some people through public construction jobs building roads, schools,

municipal buildings, and parks. Many Rhode Islanders—like Rose Island's Jesse, Charlie, and Paul—grew vegetable gardens to supplement their food supply, and the government established bread lines (or fish lines—such as the one in the photograph at left) to feed the needy, but it would take the economic boom caused by the onset of World War II in 1939 to fully pull the United States and the rest of the world out of the Great Depression.

THE RUSTY STOVE

Paul ran full-speed across the freshly-mown lighthouse lawn and burst through the kitchen door. "Gramp, the Lighthouse Service tender is headed this way!"

Both Grandpa Orton and Assistant Keeper Charlie looked up from the white, blue, and green nautical chart spread across the kitchen table. They'd been noting the revised placement of the channel markers used to guide ships through the mouth of the bay. "Inspector Yeates is on his way here?" Gramp asked. "Are you sure?"

Paul nodded rapidly. "Did I see him first?" His grandfather had promised him fifty cents as a reward if he was the first one to spot the inspector in his boat on the way to Rose Island for a surprise check of the lighthouse.

Charlie peered through the tall window near the table. "He's right, Jesse. I can see the tender passing Castle Hill Light right now. Yeates will be here in fifteen minutes."

"Well then," Gramp said, slipping his arms into his uniform jacket and rolling up the chart. "We'd better make sure this place is spick-and-span. Not a moment to lose." He pulled two quarters from his trouser pocket and placed them in Paul's small hand. "Good work, son."

Paul admired the shiny coins with a standing lady on their front and a flying eagle on their reverse. "Thank you!" He imagined all of the chewy red licorice shoelaces he'd buy with the money on their next trip into Newport.

"Oh, no!" Charlie pointed to the lighthouse's cast iron coal stove. "With all of the work we've been doing on the boats and the channel markers, I haven't had a chance to blacken the stove lately." All three of them frowned at the brown-red spots of rust, especially noticeable around the four burners. "Yeates is sure to give us a bad mark for that. Last month, he reprimanded us because the coffee pot was a little tarnished, and this is far worse."

Gramp shook his head. "Not much can be done about it now. No time."

"I have an idea," Charlie said. He looked at Paul. "Do you know how to light a fire in the stove?"

Paul nodded hesitantly. "I think so…"

"Good." Charlie went to the pantry and returned carrying a stack of large cast-iron pots and lids. He plunked one black pot on each of the stove's four burners. "Light the stove, fill the pots with water, throw in some vegetables—like carrots, onions, and potatoes—and then close the lids."

Gramp asked, "What in the world are you up to, Charlie?"

"You'll see," Charlie said. He smiled at Paul. "Hurry!"

The two men rushed toward the lighthouse tower, leaving Paul alone in the kitchen. He quickly wadded up several sheets of newspaper and shoved them through the door of the stove followed by a few pieces of wood kindling from the wicker basket on the floor. While biting his bottom lip, he scraped a match across the side of the stove—just the way he'd seen Charlie do it a hundred times—and gasped when it erupted into a small yellow flame. Touching the match to the crumpled newspaper, he smiled when he saw the fire catch. Once the wood was burning brightly, Paul dumped a few shovelfuls of coal into the stove and closed the door. Then, using the water hand pump in the pantry, he hurriedly used a jug to fill the cooking pots on the stove. He threw in piles of carrots, potatoes, and onions and slammed shut the heavy lids just as the inspector knocked on the kitchen door, a clipboard tucked securely under one arm.

Paul opened the door and snapped a salute, just the way one of the Fort Hamilton Navy officers had taught him.

Inspector Yeates smiled kindly as his eyes swept across the blue sailor's suit Paul's mamma had lovingly made for him. "What an official welcome. I feel quite honored."

"Hello, Inspector," Gramp said, striding into the kitchen with Charlie close on his heels. "Let us show you the modifications we've made to the foghorn since the last time you were here." The two lighthouse keepers hustled the inspector outside and around the corner to the brick foghorn building at the west end of the bastion, while Paul stayed behind and periodically shoveled coal into the cooking stove. A half-hour later, when the three men returned to the kitchen, the pots were boiling and the lighthouse was filled with the delicious aroma of cooking vegetables.

Inspector Yeates nodded toward Paul. "The boy is a snappy dresser and he cooks, too?"

Charlie said, "It's just us three bachelors here, now. We all have to do our share of the housework." He winked at Paul. "We have company coming for supper tonight, so Paul here is cooking up some grub for all of us."

"Well, it smells tasty." The inspector picked up the coffee pot Paul had just carefully polished, put it down, and then signed his name to a piece of paper that he pulled from his clipboard and handed to Charlie. Smiling, Inspector Yeates said, "I only wish I had time to stay for supper."

Gramp clapped a hand on the inspector's shoulder. "Let me walk you down to the pier."

Charlie shut the door behind the two men, grabbed up the report form, and scanned it. Grinning, he collapsed into a kitchen chair. "The inspector wrote, 'The lighthouse and its premises are in shipshape condition. No deficiencies.' So, he didn't notice the rusty stove. Thanks to you, we got away with it."

Paul smiled, glad that he'd been able to help.

"And we have plenty of soup to eat all week."

Both of them laughed for a long time.

LIFE IN THE 1930s

Because Gramp, Charlie, and Paul were isolated on Rose Island, they lacked access to some modern conveniences that were becoming more readily available throughout America at that time. By 1930, 80% of the nation's homes in cities and towns were electrified, even though only about 10% of rural homes and farms had power. However, in 1935, as part of his New Deal, President Roosevelt created the Rural Electrification Administration, which provided funds to build a nationwide power infrastructure, so by 1939, 25% of those rural homes and farms were electrified, too. Residential indoor plumbing also became more widespread. By the end of the 1930s, more than half the houses in the United States contained piped hot water, a built-in bathtub or shower, and a flush toilet, all conveniences that were not available at the Rose Island Lighthouse until much later.

Despite the severe economic downturn of the Great Depression, the modernization of the United States continued to progress. In the 1930s, electronic products were introduced into the American home in the form of convenient kitchen appliances like gas stoves and electric refrigerators, washing machines, irons, and vacuum cleaners. By 1935, sales of electric refrigerators alone rose to 1.6 million per year. These more efficient appliances were especially helpful to Depression-era homemakers because homemakers could buy buy their produce and meats in bulk and keep them fresh in their new electric refrigerators.

By 1929, approximately 26 million cars traveled the American roads. In the early 1930s, due to the Depression, many car owners were very guarded with their finances and delayed purchasing new cars, driving their old ones longer. By 1933, families were experiencing improved finances, so car manufacturers began tempting them with new, more appealing cars. These models sported beautiful curved lines with

rounded steel roofs and came in attractive colors—not just the traditional black. Also, they were equipped with more powerful engines, making them more fun to drive. Car companies allowed customers to buy automobiles on credit and thus avoid the need to pay the entire amount at the time of the purchase so that by 1937 the number of cars on American roads had increased to 29 million.

Clothing fashions also changed dramatically during the Depression. Most women of that time were adequately skilled in sewing so very few clothes were store-bought. Feed-sack clothes became a popular trend of the decade, with women transforming cotton sacks into dresses, underwear, and items for the home such as curtains and towels. To accommodate this fad, some flour and feed manufacturers switched to sacks with appealing, colorful designs so they could be reused as attractive fabrics for clothing and housewares. Women in the 1930s still wanted to look smart when going out, however. An afternoon tea might call for a dress of silk or rayon crepe with puffed sleeves and a belted waist—homemade or bought second-hand—with a hat and gloves added as attractive, inexpensive accessories. For men, fashionable suits with padded shoulders and tapered sleeves—also homemade or bought second-hand—were popular for an evening out, but the average man wore work clothes most days.

KEEPING THE LIGHT BURNING

At 7 a.m. every weekday morning, a Marine launch arrived at Rose Island's pier to pick up the half-dozen soldiers who guarded Fort Hamilton overnight. Beginning the day after Labor Day, Paul joined the Marines on their short boat ride back to Newport so he could attend first-grade class at the Coggeshall Elementary School. His teacher, Miss Brown, was very nice and Paul enjoyed playing with the other children on the playground at recess, but mostly he looked forward to Charlie picking him up in the lighthouse boat at 3 p.m. and bringing him back to Rose Island. While the other kids at school complained about their afterschool chores and their pesky brothers and sisters at home, Paul was excited about the work waiting for him to do at the lighthouse.

A few afternoons a week, Paul spent an hour or so helping Gramp and Charlie cart kerosene up to the lighthouse tower and down to the foghorn building, since both the lighthouse's lantern and the foghorn's steam boiler were powered by kerosene. Hauling the fuel was hard work. The three of them filled tin pails from the big kerosene tanks located next to the Green House. Although Paul carried a 1-gallon pail instead of the 5-gallon ones used by Gramp and Charlie, it still felt like it weighed a ton. They lugged one load of kerosene through the lighthouse front door and up the steep stairs to the service room on the third story of the tower. Two more loads of kerosene were carried around the back of the lighthouse and down the dozen stairs to the brick foghorn building. This provided enough fuel to run the equipment for about two days.

Gramp often let Paul help light and tend the lighthouse beacon. To light it, one of them cranked the air pump that forced the kerosene to flow through a pipe from the third-floor reservoir up to the fourth-floor lantern room where the beacon

was housed. Then, Gramp opened the door of the lamp (the device that held the flame), which was inside the Fresnel lens (the bumpy, glass housing that surrounded the lighthouse lamp and focused its light). The Rose Island Lighthouse lamp was made of red glass that made the beam appear red, so sailors could distinguish its colored signal from those of other lighthouses. Gramp lit the lamp with a torch, closed the door, and adjusted the knob on the kerosene, making the beacon shine brightly. If the light went out during the night, an alarm system he'd invented and installed rang a loud bell in both Gramp's and Charlie's quarters, and one of them rushed up to the lantern room and relight the beacon.

Every morning at sunrise, Gramp extinguished the light, ate breakfast, and then immediately began cleaning and preparing the beacon for use that evening. With Paul's help, he checked the fuel oil level, took apart the beacon, cleaned out the piping, and then polished every surface, including the lamp, Fresnel lens, and the eight enormous panes of glass that surrounded the lantern room and protected it from the harsh New England weather.

One evening in early October just before dusk, Paul and Gramp stood in the lantern room, the light from the beacon making Gramp's white hair look pink. They waved at passengers on the deck of a passing steamship as her captain tooted the horn. The setting sun cast a golden hue on the shore and water alike, making the bay look like an enchanted fairyland, especially from their vantage point high in the lighthouse tower.

Paul said, "In school today, Frankie Tefft was bragging about how he was going to help his dad drive a farm tractor this afternoon to pick some corn. That

might have been fun, but he probably didn't get to see anything like this."

    Gramp smiled. "Chances are, you're correct about that, my boy. Few people are as fortunate as you and me."

    The two of them contentedly sighed in unison.

FRESNEL LENS

In 1822, a French physicist named Augustin Jean Fresnel (pronounced: fray-NEL) proposed the design of a new lens that would revolutionize lighthouse beacons throughout the world. His invention, which became known as the Fresnel lens, took light from a traditional source, such as a kerosene lantern, and amplified it so that it would beam a much greater distance. Before, a lighthouse beacon could be seen a maximum distance of 12 miles, but with the addition of a Fresnel lens, that same beacon was now visible all the way to the horizon, 20 miles away.

As part of his invention, Augustin Fresnel also devised a way that the lens of each lighthouse could rotate at a given speed, which would cause the beam to appear to flash at a specific rate when viewed from a fixed point. And the beam could be colored, too—often red or green—by using a tinted glass shade on the kerosene lantern housed inside the Fresnel lens. The color and frequency of flashing of a lighthouse beam are called its characteristics and are different for each lighthouse, allowing a ship's captain to distinguish one lighthouse from another and thus to more accurately fix his position. Originally, the Rose Island Lighthouse housed a sixth-order Fresnel lens that broadcast a steady, non-flashing red beam of light. In 1993, the lighthouse was renovated and an electronic 6-second flashing white light was installed, which was replaced with a replica polycarbonate sixth-order Fresnel lens in 2013, during the second phase of the restoration project.

A Fresnel lens is made of many glass prisms held together in a brass framework. The prisms bend and magnify the light from a lantern mounted inside the lens, concentrating the rays into one, powerful beam. Fresnel lenses come in six different sizes, called orders, that range in dimensions. The largest is the first-order lens that may be as much as 6 feet wide and 12 feet high and is used in the tallest ocean lighthouses for maximum visibility. On the other end of the size spectrum is the sixth-order Fresnel lens, which is only about 1 foot wide and 2 feet tall and is utilized in smaller lighthouses such as those found in harbors and channels.

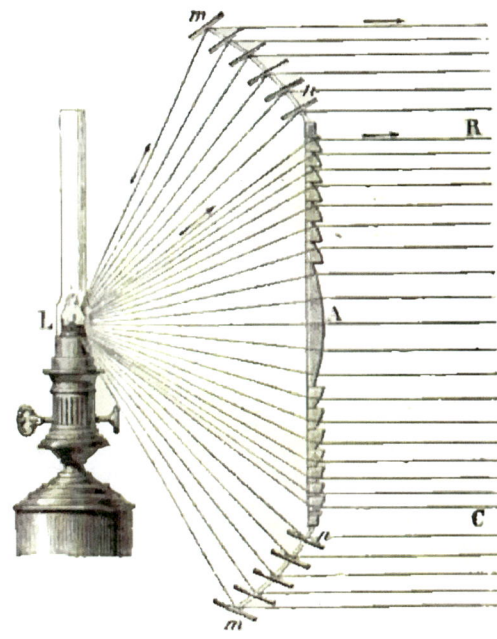

A FOGGY NIGHT

One foggy night a few weeks before Thanksgiving, Paul couldn't sleep. His bedroom was located immediately adjacent to the foghorn house, so when the deafening double-blast of the steam horn sounded at fifteen-second intervals, everything in Paul's room vibrated violently and his windows rattled noisily in their frames. Yawning, he put on his winter coat, hat, and boots, and tromped out into the cold and down the stairs to the foghorn building, where he found Charlie tending to the equipment.

"Well, hello there, old sport," Charlie said with a smile. "Come on over here, stuff this cotton in your ears, and I'll show you how this all works." Gramp was the Rose Island Lighthouse Keeper, in charge of the entire station, but Charlie Eldridge was the Assistant Lighthouse Keeper, so maintaining the foghorn was one of his chief responsibilities. He pointed out the various pieces of equipment to Paul, pausing every fifteen seconds while the foghorn bellowed.

Charlie explained that the foghorn building held two of everything: boilers, steam engines, pressure tanks, pipes, valves, clockworks, and even foghorns, all arranged side-by-side and polished to a high gleam. He called it a redundant system and said if one of the pieces of equipment didn't work correctly, they used its twin to sound the horn in foggy conditions. Charlie said if both of the foghorn systems failed at the same time—which happened rarely—he wound the clockwork attached to the big, old fog bell that stood on the rocks outside the building causing it to ring, a double-strike every fifteen seconds until the fog lifted.

"But why do we blow the horn or ring the bell?" Paul asked. "How does that help the ships' captains?"

"When it's foggy, like tonight, the captains can't see the lighthouse beacons very well. So instead, they listen for the fog signals from Rose Island and from the other lighthouses in the area—like Beavertail and Castle Hill—to determine exactly where their ships are in the bay. Then they look at their charts to figure out what hazards they need to avoid." He pointed down toward the water. "Like the rocks at the base of the bastion here or the sandbar at the north end of the island. If a ship ran into something like that, it could cause a lot of damage, or even sink the ship."

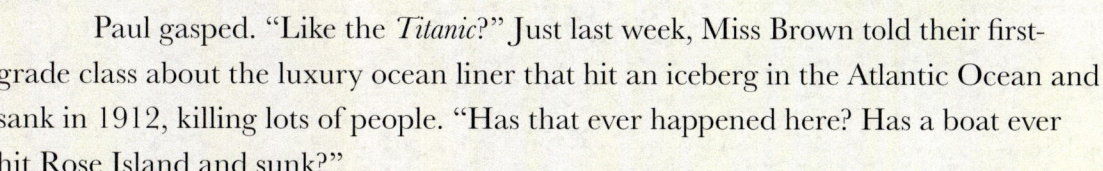

Paul gasped. "Like the *Titanic*?" Just last week, Miss Brown told their first-grade class about the luxury ocean liner that hit an iceberg in the Atlantic Ocean and sank in 1912, killing lots of people. "Has that ever happened here? Has a boat ever hit Rose Island and sunk?"

"I only know of one ship that ever hit the island—the SS *Plymouth*—but she didn't sink."

"What happened?" Paul asked. "Can you tell me the story?"

Charlie tousled the boy's hair. "Okay. Let's go sit by the stove where it's warmer." They drew up a chair on either side of the black pot-bellied stove in the corner of the room. Charlie poured two mugs of hot cocoa from a thermos and began, "Back in June of 1894, the Fall River Steamship Line had a new, fancy passenger steamship ship—the SS *Priscilla*—that they wanted to show off."

"You said you were going to talk about the *Plymouth*, not the *Priscilla*," Paul

said with a frown.

Charlie chuckled. "Who's telling this story? You or me?"

"Sorry." Paul sipped his cocoa.

"As I was saying, the *Priscilla* was the biggest sidewheel steamship built, designed to carry 1,500 passengers back and forth from Fall River to New York City in luxurious accommodations that included delicious food and beautiful cabins. On its first day of service, the steamship company planned a big celebration in Newport, complete with a brass band and a parade. The only problem was that by the time they were supposed to launch the *Priscilla*, very dense fog had rolled in across the bay and word came from the Coast Guard that the *Plymouth* had run aground at the south end of Rose Island—"

"That's right there!" Paul pointed toward the door of the foghorn building.

"Exactly. That night the captain of the *Plymouth* got lost in the fog, mistakenly thought he was already at Fort Adams, turned too early, and sailed the ship onto the reef here at Rose Island. Even with two tugboats, they couldn't pull her off. They had to offload the passengers and the freight onto another steamer, ferry them back to Newport, and put them on a train to New York City. By that time, it was too late to do the big ceremonial launching of the *Priscilla*, so they postponed it to another day."

"But nobody on the *Plymouth* got hurt or drownded?" Paul asked.

"Nope. No one got so much as a scratch. The next day at high tide, the salvage crew pulled the ship off the reef and towed her back to Fall River for repairs." He added, "And there haven't been any shipwrecks on Rose Island since then."

Paul puffed out a breath of relief. "Good. But you better get back to work now and make sure the foghorn keeps working tonight." He pulled his hat down over his ears and marched back to his bedroom, now glad to hear the blasts of the foghorn since he knew their purpose.

FOG SIGNALS

Fifteen years after the Rose Island Lighthouse was built in 1870, a timber A-framed bell tower supporting a 1,000-pound cast iron bell was added on the rocks on the west side of the building to be used in foggy weather. The bell was equipped with a clockwork system that, when wound and operated, caused a mallet to strike the bell twice every fifteen seconds, Rose Island's unique, identifiable fog signal. This bell, like all other lighthouse bells in the area, served two purposes during periods of limited visibility due to fog: to help mariners locate their positions relative to the various lighthouses within Narragansett Bay and to warn ships of potential dangers (reefs, sandbars, shoals, etc.). Since the bay was frequently blanketed by fog—up to 10 days per month during the summer—the bell saw much use.

In 1912, a brick building was built on the rocks below the west side of the Rose Island Lighthouse, which housed a new steam-powered foghorn system that replaced the bell system, although the bell itself was retained in case of emergency. As Charlie explained to Paul, the foghorn system was designed with redundancy with two of every piece of apparatus so that if one piece failed, its twin could be called into service. To sound the fog signal, the system employed Daboll trumpets invented by Celadon Leeds Daboll of New London, Connecticut. For each trumpet, a coal-fired engine was used to compress air into a cylinder where it was then forced through a narrow opening, past the horn's reed, causing the reed to vibrate. This was similar to the way a clarinet reed functions; however, the Daboll trumpet reed was steel and much larger: 10 inches long and 2.25 inches wide.

The Rose Island Lighthouse's foghorns were elevated to increase their range by affixing them to the roof of the foghorn building. To provide a sufficient head of steam to power up the fog alert system each time, coal had to be continuously fed into the engine for 10 minutes or more. After that, one ton of coal was required for every ten hours of operation. In 1912, Julius Johansen was hired as Rose Island Lighthouse's first assistant keeper, in part to help with the extra workload created by the new fog signal. He joined Head Keeper Charles S. Curtis, who had been in charge of the lighthouse since 1887. When the fog rolled in, they alternated four-hour shifts of shoveling coal into the foghorn's engine—exhausting work. Eventually, the coal engine was converted to operate using kerosene, making the process somewhat easier; however, the kerosene still had to be carried to the engine, and the foghorn equipment required constant cleaning and repair.

Fog signals had limitations. During periods of fog, cold and warm air layers cause the sound to deflect, skip, bounce, echo, and sometimes be silenced altogether, so that the sound from a fog signal might be heard at one mile, not at two miles, and then again at three. Or perhaps the sound might seem to come from one direction, when in fact it originated from another. Before the days of sonar and radar, a mariner had no way to determine his exact distance from the lighthouse issuing the fog signal, even though each lighthouse's signal was rated for a certain range. Until technology advanced, however, fog signals offered a sailor his best chance of avoiding navigational hazards in foggy conditions.

COFFEE TRADING

Every day, regardless of the weather, Rose Island Lighthouse Keeper Jesse Orton walked around the island to survey the beaches and nearby bay for signs of trouble. And every day, when he wasn't at school, Paul joined Gramp on his walk. For one of these tours in mid-February, a Nor'easter was blowing across the island with bone-chilling cold, so Paul and Gramp bundled themselves in their warmest coats, hats, mittens, and boots. As they passed through the lighthouse kitchen, Gramp slung a canvas bag over his shoulder.

"What's in there today?" Paul asked.

"The usual," Gramp said. "Plus, some jars of those beets we canned in August. Do you suppose sailors like beets?"

"I sure hope so."

Paul and Gramp tramped out into the cold and headed toward the northern tip of the island. As they crunched over the frozen grass, a voice called out, "Hello, Paulie! Be careful not to get blown off the island today!"

Paul turned and waved to a sailor standing near the Southwest Gun Mount. He liked how the Navy guys often treated him like their little brother, which made him miss Pappa and Mamma a little less. He hadn't seen his parents since Christmastime.

As Paul and Gramp passed the Northwest Bastion on the west side of the island, Gramp pointed across the bay toward Jamestown. "Good thing they used an extra tug for that barge. And some additional lines. Even then, she's giving them some difficulty. We should keep an eye on them, just in case." Paul looked to see two tugboats dragging a heavily loaded coal barge through the bay. Despite its large size, the barge was bobbing up and down in the white-tipped waves like a toy boat in a stream.

At the northernmost tip of Rose Island, Paul spotted a small boat with a jagged hole in her hull washed up on the rocks. "Looks like a dinghy that tore loose from somewhere," Gramp said. "It has no identification on it, but I'll list it in my report. Maybe someone will come looking for it."

They rounded the end of the island and started down its east side where the wind was a little calmer, passing several Naval Torpedo Station buildings on their right. "What are those buildings used for?"

Gramp pointed toward another, larger brick and concrete building at the southeast tip of the island. "In that building by the pier, men put explosives into torpedoes. Once the torpedoes are loaded, they are stored in these buildings here. See the iron carts sitting on the train tracks that run into the buildings?"

Paul nodded.

"Those are used to move the torpedoes around the island, and then to transport them to the pier when it's time to load them onto ships."

"Why are the men making torpedoes?" Paul asked. "Is our country fighting with another country again?" He had heard Pappa and Mamma talk about the Great War that had happened before he was born, in which lots of men from many different countries fought and died. He didn't want Pappa or Gramp to have to fight—and maybe die—in a war like that.

Gramp smiled. "Hopefully our country will never be in another war again. But our government is making torpedoes and other weapons, just in case."

After scoping out the eastern and southern shores of the island and finding nothing amiss, They hiked up a small hill and entered the Officers' Quarters. Paul was glad to be out of the cold, even if only for a few minutes.

Gramp knocked on the door of a small office and they were waved inside by a smiling man in a tan uniform. "Captain Orton and Master Paul, good to see you. I was afraid you might skip your visit today due to the cold."

Gramp chuckled. "Officer Andrews, it would take a lot more than a little

Nor'easter to keep us away from the chance to get some more coffee. We used up the last of our supply this morning and I don't fancy facing Charlie tomorrow unless I'm able to lay in a fresh supply." He pulled two bottles of fresh milk, two dozen eggs, and four big jars of beets from his canvas bag.

"Fresh milk and eggs…good. And beets?" Officer Andrews said. "I can't remember the last time we had those. I'm sure the guys will love them." He placed four tins of coffee on his desk. "That should last you for a little while."

"Thank you very much," Gramp said. "Are you sure you can spare them? Coffee's hard to find during this Depression."

"For some reason, they keep sending us extra coffee with every food shipment. I guess they want to make sure we don't fall asleep on the job here at Rose Island."

"That would never happen," Gramp said, tucking the coffee into his canvas bag.

"How about you, young man?" Officer Andrews asked Paul. "Does your grandpa ever let you have a cup of coffee, too? Or are you too young?"

"I get a cup every morning," Paul said. "He even gives some to Buddy, the dog."

"With a heavy dose of milk," Gramp added with a smile. "For both of them."

"Well, then, if all four of you at the lighthouse drink coffee, it's a good thing we were able to refresh your supply."

Paul and Gramp rebuttoned their coats and pulled their hats down over their ears. "Thanks again, Officer Andrews," Gramp said. "See you tomorrow."

"Until tomorrow."

NEWPORT NAVAL TORPEDO STATION

The Rose Island torpedo-making facilities Paul and Gramp passed on their daily walks were part of the Newport Naval Torpedo Station (NNTS), which had a long history in Narragansett Bay. The station was originally established on nearby Goat Island in 1869 to develop and test torpedoes and other explosive devices. At first, the station's work focused on mines and spar torpedoes, which were attached to the end of a pole, rammed into an enemy's vessel, and then detonated. The facility also manufactured explosives and designed systems that could propel torpedoes through the water.

In the early 1900s, NNTS began actually building torpedoes, but this work was interrupted during World War I, when production switched to the manufacture of mines, depth charges, and bombs, deemed

more crucial to the war effort. To support this increased weapon production, the station was expanded to include facilities on neighboring Gould Island and Rose Island. On Rose Island, this prompted the construction of supplementary buildings for use as magazines (storage facilities for explosives) and places to fill torpedo warheads. Also, gun mounts, a blast wall, sea walls, and staff housing were added, along with a water tower and electrical service.

After the war, NNTS returned to the development and construction of torpedoes, focusing on those used on ships. When the Navy introduced its first torpedo planes in the 1920s, the station was responsible for the redesign of existing torpedoes so they could be dropped from aircraft. The station's manufacturing activity increased as global tensions escalated, and, when the United States entered World War II in 1941, NNTS was an important contributor to wartime weapon production. In fact, three different varieties of torpedoes made in Newport were selected as the standard weapons for aircraft, submarines, and destroyers.

When World War II ended in 1945, NNTS stepped down its weapon production, halting completely by 1946, when the station switched back to torpedo research, design, and storage. In December 1951, the Goat Island station and its satellite facilities were officially decommissioned and their research and development activities were transferred to a facility in nearby Coddington Cove and placed under a new command, designated the Newport Naval Underwater Ordnance Station.

A STRANGE VISITOR

After school one spring afternoon, Paul was sitting on the lighthouse's living room sofa, eating a warm peanut butter cookie—freshly made by Charlie—and drinking a cold glass of Bessie's milk, when he thought he saw something just outside the window. He stopped chewing for a moment and stared intently but spied only gentle waves rolling in from the ocean. "I must be seeing things," he told Buddy.

The dog wagged his tail and inched closer to Paul's half-eaten cookie.

But then Paul saw the same thing again: a dark-haired man with his hands cupped around his face and his nose pressed against the outside of the window, peering into the lighthouse.

"Gramp!" Paul yelped. He sprang from the sofa and raced up the stairs to the lighthouse tower, colliding with his grandpa on the upper landing. Buddy barked at them from the first floor.

"What is it, my boy?" Gramp asked Paul, chuckling. "You look as if you've seen a ghost."

Paul grabbed his grandpa's hand and towed him back down to the living room. Pointing toward the window with a shaking finger, he said, "Out there! A man!"

"Where? In the water?" Gramp intently scanned the waves.

"No. Looking in the window at me."

"Truly?" Gramp quickly strode to the window and looked down into the yard. "I don't see anyone, but let's go outside and check, shall we?"

Paul and Buddy followed him out the kitchen door and around the corner of the building, where they came upon a man sitting hunched over on the back stoop. Right away, Paul noticed two odd things about the man: he was dripping wet from head to toe and he was completely naked.

Gramp stroked his mustache. Nodding to the man, he said, "Hello, my good sir. What seems to be your…er…difficulty?"

The man brushed his wet hair away from his bloodshot eyes and looked up at them. "Fell off the steamship and swam ashore."

Buddy sniffed the man's wet toes and then sneezed several times.

Paul noticed the man swayed a bit when he talked and his breath smelled funny—almost like aftershave.

Gramp nodded. "I saw the *Plymouth* go by about a half-hour ago. Didn't notice anybody falling overboard; I must have missed that. And…er…your clothes?"

"I don't swim all that good, so I took 'em off. I was afeared of drowning."

"I see." Gramp turned to Paul. "Run inside and grab my gray raincoat from the hook in the pantry. Get my old pair of galoshes, too."

Gramp tossed the raincoat over the man's shoulders and he and Paul looked away as the man buttoned it up and slipped his feet into the too-big shoes.

"I imagine you'd like a lift back to the mainland?" Gramp asked.

"If it wouldn't be too much of a bother." The man leaned hard against the railing and clutched his stomach. Paul wondered if he might be sick.

Gramp consulted his gold pocket watch. "As it so happens, the Marine launch is due here in a few minutes to drop off tonight's guard patrol. Let's see if you can catch a ride into Newport with them." The three of them crunched down the clamshell path to the nearby Officers' Quarters building while Buddy stayed at the lighthouse.

Standing at the administration desk, Gramp explained the situation to Sergeant Murphy, who broke into a loud guffaw of laughter. He called several other Marines over and had Gramp repeat the story for them. Pretty soon, Gramp, Paul, and the man from the steamship were surrounded by a group of young Marines, doubled over with laughter, making funny comments about the fellow's awkward predicament. After a full two minutes of this, the man seemed to have had enough. He picked up a heavy black flashlight off the sergeant's desk and threw it, denting a hole in the bottom of a door.

The smiles instantly vanished from the faces of the Marines as two of them grabbed the man and pinned his arms behind him.

"We'll have none of that," Sergeant Murphy said sternly. He sniffed the man's breath. "Were you by any chance imbibing any alcoholic beverages before or during your brief journey on the steamship?"

The man shrugged. "I might have had a couple of shots."

"A couple?" Sergeant Murphy jerked his chin toward the door. "Take him down to the launch."

Two Marines escorted the man toward the pier.

Looking at Gramp, the sergeant said, "Thanks, Jesse. We'll take care of him."

Back at the lighthouse, Paul helped Gramp prepare dinner while Buddy snoozed in his customary spot under the kitchen table. As Gramp dished out steaming plates of chicken and noodles, he chuckled and shook his head. "Well, well, well, my boy. That was something you certainly don't see every day, something you can tell your grandkids about."

FALL RIVER LINE

From 1847 to 1937, the Fall River Line was one of the most popular means of transportation between New England and New York City. Founded by Massachusetts businessman, Colonel Richard Bordon, the line featured non-stop railway service between Boston and Fall River and then exclusive steamship service between there and the line's Hudson River dock in Manhattan. The company arranged its schedules so that the trains or ships arrived at their destination city—Boston or New York City—in the early morning, thus allowing passengers a full day for business or shopping, before departing in the early evening for an overnight journey home. Two steamships serviced the 8- to 10-hour water leg of the journey. When one was in New York City, the other was in Fall River, thus providing nightly service in both directions. The Fall River Line trains were known for being clean and on-time and their passenger ships, which sailed past Rose Island, were the most advanced and luxurious ships of that era.

In 1883, the Fall River Line launched the *Pilgrim*, the largest steamship in the world at that time. The sleek white ship with twin black funnels was 374 feet long, had a double hull for increased safety, and provided sleeping quarters for 1,200 passengers. With its 6,500-horsepower engine, the *Pilgrim* often made the 175-mile trip between Fall River and New York in less than 9 hours. Other flagships were added to the company's fleet over the years and each one was larger and more elegant than the last. In 1894, the luxurious *Priscilla* was added to the line. Capable of accommodating 1,500 passengers, she boasted electric lights in the passenger lounges and her 360 staterooms. Her two-story grand saloon had a tinted-glass chandelier and a clerestory dome. The steamship, *Commonwealth*, launched in 1908, was the grandest ship of the fleet. She was 438 feet long, provided 425 staterooms, and featured a grand staircase, a dining saloon, and a dance floor, each equally elaborate as those found in much larger ocean-going liners.

Over its long history, the Fall River Line transported several United States presidents including Arthur, Harrison, Cleveland, and both Roosevelts, as well as other notables such as millionaires, socialites, and movie stars. However, its reasonable fares made it a favorite mode of transportation for honeymooners, vacationers, and average travelers, too. Often referred to as floating palaces, the ships of the Fall River Line permitted all passengers to experience a few hours of travel luxury.

POEMS WITH GRAMP

As the end of the school year approached, Paul's ability to read and write increased greatly. He often pestered Gramp or Charlie to help him read some of the books standing on the lighthouse's bookshelves. One afternoon in May, Gramp was sitting in the warm sunshine on the bench outside the kitchen door, writing in a leather-bound notebook when Paul hopped down the lighthouse stairs carrying a thick, black book. "Please help me read this."

Gramp looked at the book's spine. "*War and Peace* by Leo Tolstoy. Humm. My boy, I think this one may be a bit difficult for you to understand."

Paul's face fell in disappointment.

"Tell you what," Gramp said, "how about if instead of us reading this, I teach you how to write a poem?"

Paul squinched up his nose. "I don't like poems."

"Why do you say that?"

"Miss Brown reads poems to us at school sometimes—about flowers and love and icky stuff like that."

Gramp nodded thoughtfully. "It's true that some poems are about flowers and love. But people have written many other poems about things you might find more interesting."

"Really? Like what?"

"Have you ever heard a cowboy poem?"

Paul's mouth dropped open. "Written by a real cowboy?" Back in New York, Pappa sometimes read him exciting cowboy tales from *Western Story Magazine*. Paul wanted to be a cowboy when he grew up. Or a lighthouse keeper. He wasn't sure which.

Grandpa said, "This is part of a cowboy poem written by a man named Charles Badger Clark:"

```
          Oh, for me a horse and saddle
          Every day without a change;
          With the desert sun a-blazin'
          On a hundred miles o' range.

          Just a-ridin', just a-ridin',
          Desert ripplin' in the sun,
          Mountains blue along the skyline—
          I don't envy anyone.
```

"Wow. That's not icky at all," Paul said.

Gramp held up his notebook. "This is full of poems that I've written, and I'm pretty sure none of them are icky, either. Most of them are about life here on Rose Island. Some of them are even about you."

"Would you read one to me?"

Gramp nodded. "But first, why don't you write a new poem of your own?"

"I don't know how."

"I'll help you. First of all, you must decide what you want your poem to be about."

Paul smiled. "That's easy. I want to write about living here at the lighthouse with you."

"Okay." Gramp opened his notebook to a blank page. "Tell me some of the things you'd like to talk about in your poem."

"The birds—mostly seagulls—and how they fly around and then land and watch us."

Gramp wrote some notes with his pencil. "What else?"

"And you, Charlie, and Buddy, and how you all take good care of me."

Gramp scribbled more in his notebook. "Anything else?"

Paul pointed toward the pasture. "Bessie, and the chickens, and the garden: how they give us all milk and eggs and vegetables to eat." He looked up at the lighthouse. "And the beacon and foghorn, and how they keep ships safe at night and in the fog."

Gramp nodded as he jotted more notes. "Is that it?" he asked. "Do you want to include anything else in your poem?"

Paul pondered for a moment. "Yes. I want to say how beautiful everything looks from the lantern room: the glowing islands, the sparkling water, and the pretty boats sailing by."

"Okay." Gramp wrote a few more words. "And what do you want to call your poem?"

Paul thought about that question. "My Home in the Lighthouse."

"Sounds like a perfect title to me." Gramp smiled. "And, just like that, you've written a poem. Let me read it to you."

>
> <u>My Home in the Lighthouse</u>
> By Paul Stedman
>
> Seagulls fly, land, and watch
> As Gramp, Charlie, and Buddy take good care of me.
>
> Bessie, the chickens, and the garden
> Give us all milk, eggs, and vegetables to eat,
> While the lighthouse beacon and foghorn
> Keep ships safe at night and in the fog.
>
> And everything looks beautiful from the lantern room:
> the glowing islands, the sparkling water,
> and the pretty boats sailing by.

Paul was amazed. "I wrote a real poem?"

Gramp nodded. "And it's a good one." He waved his notebook. "I used to read some of these poems to Gram, and she liked them." He smiled at Paul. "I'm sure she'd like yours, too, and would be very proud of you for writing it."

"With your help."

Gramp tousled Paul's hair. "They were your words, my boy; I just wrote them down."

ENTERTAINMENT IN THE 1930s

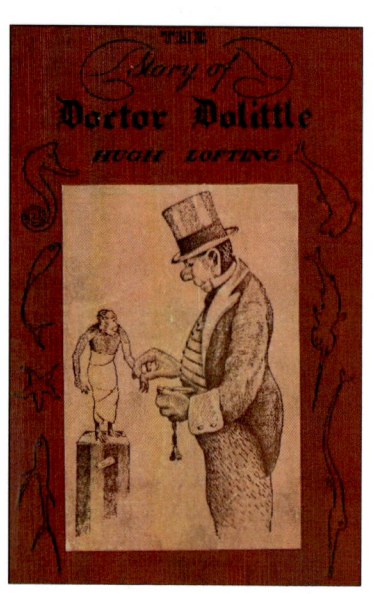

In the 1930s, the Great Depression led many Americans to seek out new kinds of entertainment to escape from their financial and economic worries. Gramp and Paul wrote poetry while other children and adults turned to books for diversion. One very popular children's book of that era was *The Story of Doctor Dolittle* by Hugh Lofting. Published in 1920, this book captivated readers with its fantastic tales of a doctor who could speak to animals like pushmi-pullyus and gigantic snails. Another often-read children's book of that time was *The Magical Land of Noom*. Written by Johhny Gurelle in 1922, it was a magical story of siblings Johnny and Janey and their grandparents who explored an enchanted world in their homemade flying machine. In the 1930s, adults might have read Dashiell Hammett's *The Maltese Falcon*, published in 1930. *Falcon* was an instant best-seller and the inspiration for all crime novels to follow. *The Good Earth* by Pearl Buck presented Chinese people in a positive light and was credited with improving many Americans' opinions of Asians. The book was the bestselling novel of 1931 and 1932, won the Pulitzer Prize in 1932, and contributed to Buck winning the Nobel Prize in 1938, making her the first American woman to win for literature.

Another popular form of entertainment during the Depression was motion pictures, newly enhanced with the addition of sound and color. Disney's first full-length animated film, *Snow White and the Seven Dwarfs*, came out in 1937, and 1939 saw the release of such classics as *The Wizard of Oz*, starring Judy Garland, and *Gone With the Wind*, featuring Clark Gable and Vivien Leigh. In the 1930s, feature movies generally lasted two hours or more and often were preceded by a newsreel and a short-feature film, making a trip to the movie theater an all-day affair.

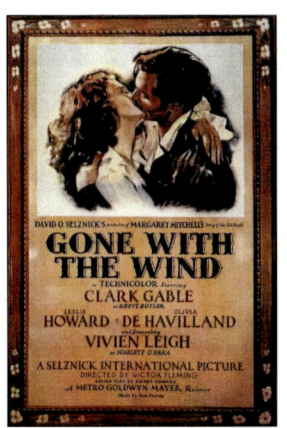

In response to the demand for novel family entertainment, some entrepreneurs invented new games. Garnet Carter of Lookout, Tennessee, came up with the idea of golf for the whole family, played on a series of small courses. When he built his first Tom Thumb Golf Course in 1929, miniature golf was born and became an instant success, with roadside franchises popping up throughout the country. Course owners provided putters and balls and created imaginative course designs with an array of unique obstacles to challenge players aiming for the cups. Because of the game's popularity, some optimists suggested the miniature golf industry might be capable of lifting the United States out of the Great Depression.

FIREWORKS WITH MAMMA AND PAPPA

And just like that, Paul's time at Rose Island came to an end. Last June, Mamma and Pappa dropped him off to stay at the lighthouse with Gramp and Charlie. Now it was the Fourth of July weekend, one year later, and his parents were back to spend a few days relaxing on the island. Then they were going to take Paul home with them to Queens, New York, so he could get resettled at home before starting second grade there in the fall.

As the sun sank closer and closer toward the hills of Jamestown, Mamma gathered the leftover food and dirty dishes from their picnic dinner and carted them back into the lighthouse's kitchen. Gramp, Pappa, and Charlie all lit pipes while Paul thumbed through the latest issue of *Western Story Magazine*, a coming-home present from Pappa. Most of the words in it were too difficult for Paul to figure out by himself, but he enjoyed looking at the colorful drawings of cowboys and their horses. He would ask Pappa to read the stories with him later.

"So, Paul, my boy," Gramp said, "what are you going to remember most about your time here with Charlie and me?"

"Rowing around in *Paul W.*," he said with a smile, pointing to the handsome white and teak dinghy pulled up on the beach below. When no one had claimed the damaged boat that washed up on the island's north beach back in February, Gramp and Charlie repaired and repainted it as a surprise for Paul, and even named the boat after him, as a thank-you for helping out at the lighthouse. Since receiving the boat a few weeks ago, the boy had spent every spare moment rowing it around Rose Island, learning how to navigate the surrounding seascape. Just this afternoon, he'd treated his father to a trip in the dinghy, pointing out all of the shore features he now knew so well after more than a year of living there.

Stretching out on the picnic blanket, Gramp said to Paul, "Just remember

Paul W. will always be here, waiting for you in the boat shed, if you ever want to come back for a visit."

"Oh, I'll be back!" Paul said emphatically. He looked at his father. "Maybe next summer?"

Pappa puffed his pipe and nodded. "Your mamma and I already talked about it. We figured now that you've had the chance to experience a bachelor's life up here with Gramp, you'll be wanting to come back every chance you can get."

"At least for a few years until I retire," Gramp added.

"Oh, you're welcome to come back after that, too," Charlie said, "especially if I'm the next lighthouse keeper. With all you've learned this year—tending the chickens, Bessie, and the garden, plus helping out with the beacon, foghorn, and other duties—any keeper would greatly appreciate your assistance."

Paul smiled a huge smile.

Charlie tapped out his pipe on the bottom of his shoe and rose to his feet. "It looks like it's going to be a clear night—no need for the foghorn—so, if it's all right with you, Jesse, I'll go get the beacon ready so you can just stay here and relax with the family."

Gramp said, "That sounds like an offer I can't refuse. But make sure you come back down at 9:00 and join us to see the fireworks over Fort Adams. Major Dennis promised a good show."

"Why are they having the fireworks tonight—on the third—instead of tomorrow?" Charlie asked.

"It's supposed to rain tomorrow," Gramp said.

"That makes good sense." Charlie passed Mamma as he headed up to the tower and she emerged from the lighthouse, carrying sweaters and blankets for everyone, with Buddy following closely behind her. At 8:22, the sundown gun sounded from Fort Adams and Charlie lit the Rose Island Lighthouse beacon, its steady red light visible all the way out to Block Island Sound. At 8:55, Charlie rejoined them on the picnic blanket, and then at 9:00 the first of the fireworks exploded over Fort Adams, only a mile away.

As the red, white, and blue bursts filled the night sky, Mamma hugged Paul. "Look, honey," she said, "Newport is throwing a goodbye party, just for you."

He giggled. "Yes, they are, but I'll be back."

And he was.

***

For most of his childhood, Paul Stedman spent his summers on Rose Island, even after Gramp was no longer the keeper there. The rest of the year, he lived with his parents in Queens, New York. Growing up, Paul attended Jamaica High School in Queens but left early to enlist in the Navy during World War II, where he served as a signalman. After the war, Paul began a 40-year career in banking. He married Dorothy McCulloch in 1950, and together they moved to Wantagh, NY, on Long Island, where they raised two children, Barbara and Geoffrey. In 1988, Paul retired and he and Dorothy moved to Bradenton, Florida, where he enjoyed golfing and frequent trips to the beach.

Throughout his life, Paul enjoyed golf, skiing, and ice skating and was on his high school hockey team. He often sang in his church's choir, loved circus music, and enjoyed spending time with his 5 grandchildren, entertaining them with stories about his boyhood times living in the Rose Island Lighthouse. Paul died in Florida in 2005, at the age of 79.